INSPIRING ARTISTS

PAUL CÉZANNE

Franklin Watts

First published in Great Britain in 2015 by
The Watts Publishing Group

Copyright © 2015 The Watts Publishing Group 2015

Editor: Julia Bird
Design: Mark Ruffle/www.rufflebrothers.co.uk
Page layout: sprout.uk.com

ISBN 978 1 4451 4546 4

Dewey number: 750
Printed in China

Franklin Watts
An imprint of
Hachette Children's Group
Part of The Watts Publishing Group
Carmelite House
50 Victoria Embankment
London EC4Y 0DZ

An Hachette UK Company
www.hachette.co.uk

www.franklinwatts.co.uk

INSPIRING ARTISTS

PAUL CÉZANNE

SUSIE BROOKS

W

FRANKLIN WATTS
LONDON•SYDNEY

CONTENTS

MAKING ART MODERN

When Paul Cézanne first exhibited his paintings, people criticised, rejected and even laughed at him. He went on to change the art world forever. His boldly coloured pictures of apples and mountains paved the way for a new approach to painting. Today Cézanne is widely celebrated as the 'father' of modern art.

ASPIRING ARTIST

Cézanne was born in Provence in southern France in 1839. His father, a wealthy banker, disapproved of his dream of becoming an artist and pressed him to study law for a while. But at the age of 22, Cézanne won the battle to apply for art school in Paris. It was there he met a set of groundbreaking painters, including Claude Monet (1840–1926) and Camille Pissarro (1830–1903) (see p.10). He also discovered the work of Old Masters in the Louvre Museum.

The Artist's Father, Reading 'L'Événement', 1866

Fields at Bellevue, 1892–1895

BACK TO NATURE

While Paris was buzzing with artistic ideas, Cézanne never really felt at home there. What inspired him was nature – especially the coastline and landscape of his native Provence, as he later captured in works such as *Fields at Bellevue* (opposite, bottom). Cézanne wanted to paint the world as no one had before, using bold blocks of colour to build up shapes. Instead of copying nature, he tried to show how we experience it, not just standing still, but with moving eyes.

Castle and Sun, Paul Klee, 1928

INSPIRING ARTIST

At the time, Cézanne's patchwork paintings came as a shock. They didn't look realistic like traditional art. But later artists began to admire Cézanne. Pablo Picasso (1881–1973) and Georges Braque (1882–1963) borrowed his ideas to develop Cubism (see p.27). Paul Klee (1879–1940) was inspired by the way he used colour and shape, and interpreted it in his own works, such as *Castle and Sun* (below). Other artists, from Piet Mondrian (1872–1944) (p.29) to Ellsworth Kelly (1923–) (p.23) translated Cézanne's vision into an even more abstract world.

MOODY BEGINNINGS

In his twenties, Cézanne painted in a dark, moody style. He used heavy outlines and thick layers of oil paint, smeared onto canvas with a palette knife. Many of the scenes he painted came from his imagination, while others were portraits or copies of masterpieces in the Louvre.

ROMANCE VS REALISM

In Paris, Cézanne discovered the work of Eugène Delacroix (1798–1863) and Gustave Courbet (1819–1877) – two artists who influenced him in different ways. Delacroix focused on colour instead of outline to create exotic, romantic images. Courbet painted ordinary, everyday subjects in a blunt, realistic way. Cézanne tried to blend both approaches in his own work.

GUTSY STYLE

Cézanne described his style as 'butch' or 'gutsy'. You can see why in a series of portraits that he painted of his uncle in a variety of costumes, including an artist's smock and a monk's

Arab Saddling his Horse, Eugène Delacroix, 1855

robe (opposite). In these paintings, the tones are harsh, with extremes of black and white. The paint is slapped on in chunky slabs in a technique known as *impasto*, giving the picture surface a texture and life of its own. Laying down paint with a palette knife instead of a brush was quite new – Cézanne had seen it in the work of Courbet. It is a technique that many artists still use today.

The Stonebreakers, Gustave Courbet, c.1850

ART SPOT *Cézanne's thick paint later developed cracks. Notice the way he used colour in the skin. How does it change if you look at it close up, then further away?*

Antoine Dominique Sauveur Aubert (born 1817), the Artist's Uncle, as a Monk, 1866

SELF DOUBT

Cézanne often worried that his art wasn't good enough – it was his great schoolfriend, the celebrated writer Émile Zola (1840–1902), who really encouraged him to paint. When Cézanne moved to Paris to study art in 1861, he was overwhelmed by the talent around him. Zola tried to support him by posing for a portrait that same year. Cézanne started one twice, but eventually tore it up before packing his bags to return to Provence. For much of his life, he shuttled back and forth between the countryside and the city.

Portrait of Émile Zola, c.1862–1864

MAKING AN IMPRESSION

Many exciting artists were working in Paris while Cézanne spent time there. Among them were Claude Monet, Camille Pissarro and Pierre-Auguste Renoir (1841–1919) – all painters in a style that became known as Impressionism. Their ideas had a big impact on Cézanne.

SPONTANEOUS STYLE

The Impressionists were shaking up the art world with a brand new approach to painting. They wanted to capture the fleeting effects of light and movement that we experience when we look at the world. They painted outdoors, using short, swift brushstrokes and unmixed colours. Often, they would paint the same scene again and again, at different times of day or in different weathers or seasons. Monet's painting below shows a glimpse of early morning as the sun rose over a French port. Its title, *Impression, Sunrise*, picked up by a critic, gave the Impressionist movement its name.

WEIGHTY MATTERS

Cézanne was excited by the Impressionists' bright colours, their down-to-earth subjects and their leap away from traditional art. But he also felt that their spontaneous style had lost sight of the weightier side of nature. He liked the structure that he'd seen in the art of the past, saying, 'I want to make of Impressionism an art as solid as that of the museums.'

Impression, Sunrise, Claude Monet, 1872

The Hanged Man's House, 1873

FIRM VS FLEETING

Notice how firmly Cézanne's trees and buildings seem anchored to the ground in *The Hanged Man's House*. His brushstrokes are densely packed, knitting together the shapes in the picture. Cézanne painted patches, or *taches*, of colour that he arranged very deliberately to balance and stabilise his scene. Compare this to Monet's *Impression, Sunrise*, where the effect is free and sketchy. Instead of painting a fixed view as Cézanne has, Monet suggests a brief, flickering moment in time.

SALON SCANDAL

Every year, an official exhibition called the Salon was held in Paris. Organisers selected what they considered the best art of the time – but work that wasn't traditional was rarely accepted. Rejected by the Salon, Monet and others put on their own art shows. When Cézanne exhibited with them in 1874 and 1877, critics laughed at his apparent lack of skill and unorthodox style. One even called him a 'madman'! Critics were equally dismissive of the Impressionists' work, comparing Monet's *Impression, Sunrise* to a sketch for a wallpaper pattern.

THE GREAT OUTDOORS

One of the greatest friends Cézanne made in Paris was Camille Pissarro. Nine years Cézanne's elder, he encouraged the younger artist to get outside to paint. The pair's first expeditions were to the countryside outside Paris. They formed a double act that lasted, on and off, for 20 years.

SEEING THE LIGHT

Pissarro opened Cézanne's eyes to the light, bright colours of nature. Cézanne abandoned his dark palette and heavy use of black, in favour of sunny yellows, pinks, blues and greens. He laid down the paint purposefully, using lots of small brushstrokes. His shapes became defined by colour, instead of thick outlines.

SENSE OF STRUCTURE

Pissarro learnt from Cézanne, too. He admired how his friend searched for order and structure in nature, as well as in the composition (layout) of his paintings. His own work became more organised. The two nudged each other in new directions, while keeping their own distinctive styles.

ART SPOT *A villager who watched the two artists once said, 'Monsieur Pissarro, when he painted, dabbed, and Monsieur Cézanne smeared.' Can you see the difference in the brushstrokes used by Cézanne (below) and Pissarro (opposite)?*

Small Houses near Pontoise, 1874

The Potato Harvest, Camille Pissarro, 1874

SAME BUT DIFFERENT

Working side by side at the same time and place, Cézanne and Pissarro created these two similar yet different paintings. While Cézanne zoomed in on the sunlit houses, Pissarro left them in the distance. Pissarro liked to paint people in his landscapes, telling a story of country life. In contrast, Cézanne saw the scenery as more important, bringing it up close and making it seem more permanent.

PORTABLE PAINTS

Cézanne and Pissarro both benefited from the invention of the metal paint tube in 1841. Before that, artists had to transport their paints in pigs' bladders. Once these were punctured, the paint dried out quite quickly. Tubed paints were collapsible, so any remaining paint was protected from the air. They were also far easier to take outside and use spontaneously. They gave open-air, or *plein-air*, painting a big boost.

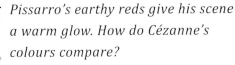 **ART SPOT** *Pissarro's earthy reds give his scene a warm glow. How do Cézanne's colours compare?*

Cézanne setting out to paint in Auvers, France, 1874

ASTONISHING APPLES

Cézanne once said, 'I will astonish Paris with an apple,' – and he was true to his word. Some of his most famous paintings are still lifes that show fruit on a table. In the past, works like this usually glimmered with realistic detail. Cézanne surprised people with his plain, unfussy approach.

MODELLING IN PAINT

In *Still Life with Apples*, we can see the same chunky brushstrokes that built up the landscape in *Small Houses near Pontoise* (see p.12). Cézanne didn't want flat apples, so he modelled them bit by bit using changes in colour. They look dense and real, but at the same time we can't forget that we are looking at a painting. This was very important to Cézanne.

Still Life with Apples, 1875–1877

CHOOSING COLOURS

Cézanne chose his palette very carefully. He knew that complementary colours, with maximum contrast, such as red and green or blue and orange, would look stronger if he placed them side by side. He used warm, bright colours to leap towards us while cooler, darker ones sink back. This helped him to create a sense of volume without relying on lines.

CAREFUL COMPOSITION

Arranging each item in a still life was an art in itself for Cézanne. He spent hours shuffling objects around, and even used coins to prop up apples at the exact angles he wanted! Cézanne looked for echoing shapes like the curves of the fruit bowl and the glass in *Still Life with Compotier* (opposite). Every fold in the cloth played a part in the composition.

Still Life with Compotier, c.1879

Woman in Front of a Still Life by Cézanne,
Paul Gauguin, 1890

ART SPOT *Which parts of* Still Life with Compotier *spring forwards and which duck back? What do you notice about the colours?*

DECORATIVE EFFECT

Unlike traditional still life painters, Cézanne ignored the textures of real life. In *Still Life with Compotier* his glass, fruits and fabrics all seem to feel the same. The overall effect is simple, yet decorative. This aspect of his work appealed to the younger artist Paul Gauguin (1848–1903), who copied the painting in the background of one of his portraits (left). You can see here how Gauguin imitated Cézanne's diagonal brushstrokes and learned from his subtle grades of colour.

15

A MODEL SUBJECT

Cézanne paid the same attention to every subject he painted – whether it was a pear or a person. Anyone who sat for a portrait would have to wait patiently while he worked for achingly long hours. His most faithful model was Hortense Fiquet, who eventually became his wife and mother of their son, Paul. There are 29 known portraits of her.

FACING PHOTOGRAPHY

At the time Cézanne was painting, artists were competing with a recent invention – photography. A portrait now had to be more than just a record of how a person looked. In Cézanne's pictures of Hortense, she is recognisable – but it is the paint itself that takes centre stage. Cézanne treats his wife as a medley of colours and shapes, rather than showing detailed features or giving away much of her character.

Madame Cézanne in a Red Armchair, c.1877

STILL VISION

In *Madame Cézanne in a Red Armchair* (below left), Hortense's hair and feet are cropped at the edge of the canvas, resembling a camera snapshot and pushing her towards us. Cézanne's patches of colour dance around the scene, yet they also make her seem still and solid. We know that Hortense's knees are the nearest thing to us – but the stripes on her skirt don't suggest that. She almost looks three dimensional and flattened at the same time.

Madame Cézanne in the Conservatory, 1891

Woman in Blue, Henri Matisse, 1937

WORKING METHOD

Madame Cézanne in the Conservatory (opposite) helps us see how Cézanne worked. He mapped out an outline, often in blue paint, then filled in the colour patch by patch. Sometimes he took as long as 20 minutes between brushstrokes – no wonder Hortense looks a bit fed up!

FUTURE FIGURES

Cézanne's handling of the human form appealed to many future painters. Henri Matisse (1869–1954) flattened shapes even further in his works such as *Woman in Blue* (above). Like Cézanne's red armchair and wallpaper, the background of this painting is as prominent as the sitter. It is as if the whole scene is part of a single pattern.

IN THE MIRROR

The only person Cézanne painted more often than his wife was himself. He posed in front of a mirror again and again, creating about 36 painted self-portraits and 26 drawn ones. Cézanne's head was bald on top – so of course it has been compared to his still life apples!

Self-Portrait and Apple, 1882–1883

SOLID SKULL

Cézanne's self-portraits reveal how he thought in three dimensions. In *Self- Portrait* (left) his head looks bulky and heavy, lit up against the dark olive-coloured wallpaper. Cézanne wove his skin out of broad patches of colour, from warm yellows and pinks to cool blues and greens. Varying the direction of his brushstrokes helped him to model the shape of his skull.

 **ART SPOT** *Cézanne's brushstrokes follow the curve of his head. How does he use colour to add to this effect? What do you notice about other shapes in this picture?*

Self-Portrait, c.1881

DISTANT MOOD

In *Self-Portrait with Palette* (below), we see Cézanne behind an easel, revealing the tools of his trade. In his right hand he holds a bunch of brushes and a palette daubed with paint. He seems distanced from us, gazing at his canvas as if completely absorbed in his work. The lines of the palette and canvas block him off like a barrier.

Self-Portrait with Palette, c.1889–1890

Self-Portrait as a Painter, Vincent van Gogh, 1888

DIFFERENT STYLE

The artist Vincent van Gogh (1853–1890) was working at the same time as Cézanne. His *Self-Portrait as a Painter* looks strikingly similar in composition. But where Cézanne used orderly strokes of paint, van Gogh put down a frenzy of smaller brush marks. One friend remembered that when the two met, Cézanne told van Gogh that he painted like a madman! Van Gogh, meanwhile, called Cézanne's style 'almost timid'. Both Cézanne and van Gogh became known as 'Post Impressionists' because they followed the Impressionists in the history of art and took on elements of their style.

LOOKING AT LANDSCAPES

Cézanne's love of the countryside constantly drew him outdoors. He wanted to capture the immensity of nature – but not in a way that others had done before. Rather than trying to show scenes we could step right into, he translated the world into mosaics of colour.

IN PERSPECTIVE

Hundreds of years before Cézanne's time, artists developed a system called perspective. This allowed them to create the illusion of space on a flat surface, using the idea that things look smaller, paler and less detailed the further away they are.

Cézanne didn't ignore the rules of perspective – but he did play with them. In his pictures he treated the background, foreground and everything else with equal importance. He wanted each shape and colour to be balanced across his canvas. He did just enough to suggest space, then let our minds add the depth.

ART SPOT *Nicolas Poussin (1594–1665) used perspective to give his pictures depth. Cézanne greatly admired this structured style of painting, but took it in his own direction. What differences can you see between this work and Cézanne's opposite?*

Landscape with a Calm, Nicolas Poussin, 1651

The Château de Medan, 1880

FLATTENING SHAPES

In Cézanne's *The Château de Medan,* the scene faces us straight on. The brushstrokes are as big and bold in the far-off fields as they are in the nearby water. The picture looks like a grid of flat shapes – Cézanne reminds us that the canvas is two-dimensional. But at the same time he uses contrasts in colour to hint at three dimensional forms.

GETTING EXPRESSIVE

Wassily Kandinsky (1866–1944) loved the way Cézanne engaged viewers' brains as well as their eyes. He flattened spaces and used vibrant brushstrokes too, making the colour take over. For Kandinsky, colour was a way to express feelings, rather than what his eyes saw. This approach became known as Expressionism.

ART SPOT *How do the colours in Kandinsky's* Winter Landscape *make you feel? Do Cézanne's paintings have an emotional impact too?*

Winter Landscape, Wassily Kandinsky, 1909

PASSION FOR PROVENCE

Nowhere was as important to Cézanne as his native Provence. He was captivated by the bright light and shadows there, and the way they defined things in the landscape. Bit by bit, he spent more time in the south of France, roaming the countryside and throwing himself into his work.

JAS DE BOUFFAN

Cézanne's father built a studio for him at their family home, Jas de Bouffan, in the 1880s. Cézanne painted dozens of pictures in and around this place. Typically he worked on several canvases at once, adding to them here and there. Other artists, including Monet and Renoir, visited and painted with him at times.

Tall Trees at the Jas de Bouffan, 1883

TREES

Cézanne regularly painted the trees near his home. *Tall Trees at the Jas de Bouffan* (below) is firmly rooted with horizontal and vertical lines, while the diagonal brushstrokes suggest movement in the branches. You can see at the bottom right how Cézanne began with thin sweeps of paint, building up his blocky colours later to create the bright and breezy effect.

SOLID SEA

The seaside village of L'Estaque was a great inspiration to Cézanne. He compared the scenery to a playing card, with coloured shapes silhouetted against each other. In *The Bay of Marseilles seen from L'Estaque* (opposite) the orange rooftops contrast with the bright blue sea, which looks dense and almost welded in paint.

ABSTRACT TAKE

The Bay of Marseilles seen from L'Estaque, c.1885

Modern artist Ellsworth Kelly saw Cézanne's *The Bay of Marseilles seen from L'Estaque* in an art gallery as a boy. He remembered the wedge of blue sea, and borrowed it for his own piece, *Lake II* (below). Many abstract artists like Kelly have been inspired by Cézanne's simplified shapes. By paring them down even further, Kelly has removed most sense of the real world.

Lake II, Ellsworth Kelly, 2002

MONUMENTAL MOUNTAINS

Cézanne longed to capture the solid, enduring side of nature. There is little more solid than a mountain, so no wonder this became one of his favourite subjects. Mont Sainte-Victoire towers majestically over Provence. Cézanne painted it more than 60 times – no two views look the same.

Montagne Sainte-Victoire, Pierre-Auguste Renoir, c.1888–1889

LEARNING THE LAND

Cézanne went on long trips to Mont Sainte-Victoire, getting to know every lump and bump. He painted it from different angles and in all weathers and seasons. Unlike the Impressionists, he merged these varied experiences into one painting. While Renoir caught a moment of blustery sunshine in his painting of the mountain (below), it feels like a moment that has come and gone. Cézanne's work feels more timeless.

NEAR AND FAR

Mont Sainte-Victoire with a Large Pine, c.1887

When Cézanne painted Mont Sainte-Victoire from a distance, he still brought it up close, drawing our eye towards it and flattening the scene as usual. Above he frames the mountain in the centre, tickled by the branches of a tree. In other works the bulky rock spans the whole width of the canvas. To Cézanne, each painting was like an experiment to record something new from nature. It is hard to see where the light is coming from in these paintings. The sky seems as concrete as the mountain, and trees and fields appear to glow on their own. This is unusual in art.

MOUNTAIN OBSESSIONS

For Japanese artist Katsushika Hokusai 1760–1849), Mount Fuji in Japan was an obsession. Like Cézanne, Hokusai enhanced the colours of his mountains and challenged traditional ways of showing space. His work had a strong influence on the Impressionists (see p.10) and other artists of the time.

 **ART SPOT** *Hokusai designed more than 140 prints of Mount Fuji. He used a technique called ukiyo-e, where shapes were cut into a wooden block, then printed onto paper. How does this look different from Cézanne's work?*

South Wind, Clear Sky (or Red Fuji), Katsushika Hokusai, c.1830

TIPPING TABLES

While outside Cézanne grappled with the changing light and weather, inside he enjoyed the constancy of still life. Just as with the mountain, he would walk around his subject and explore it from different angles. Putting these together in one scene, he made people see things in a new way.

MULTIPLE VIEWPOINTS

Look at the objects in the painting below. They all seem a bit unbalanced. We see the table from above, but the basket and pears from the side, while the high view of the floor makes it appear to slope upwards. Cézanne did this on purpose – he felt that a single viewpoint was too limited. By jumbling up the angles, he showed the way our eyes move around what we see.

SLOW PROGRESS

Cézanne was such a perfectionist that he rarely considered his paintings finished. *Kitchen Table* is one of the few canvases he actually signed. He worked so slowly that his fruits and flowers often withered and died – so he took to using fake ones as models! It could take him 100 painting sessions to complete, or abandon, a still life.

LOOK TWICE

In *Still Life with Plaster Cupid* (opposite), there's another unnaturally tilting floor. The green apple in the background is as big as the ones at the front, breaking all rules of perspective. On the left we see propped-up canvases, one of which has a still life painted on it. But is the blue cloth part of the painting, or part of this actual scene? It looks like both!

Kitchen Table (Still Life with Basket), 1888–1890

CUBIST CREATIONS

One particular group of artists picked up on Cézanne's multi-angled vision. Led by Pablo Picasso (see p.7) and Georges Braque (see p.29), they developed a style known as Cubism. *The Open Window* by Juan Gris (1887–1927) is an example of this. As you can see, Cubists rejected perspective and squashed different viewpoints onto a single shallow plane. They broke up shapes and juggled angles, challenging our eyes to make sense of a scene. They also took an interest in Cézanne's use of simplified shapes (see p.28).

Still Life with Plaster Cupid (or Plaster Cast), c.1894

The Open Window, Juan Gris, 1921

SIMPLIFYING SHAPES

Cézanne was always looking for geometry in the haphazard natural world. In a letter to a younger artist, he advised: 'Treat nature by means of the cylinder, the sphere, the cone'. By this he really meant to think of basic shapes in the things you see, and use them to organise your painting. Some artists took this idea further – to Cubism and beyond.

Turning Road at Montgeroult, c.1898

LAYERED SHAPES

You can't see cylinders, spheres or cones in *Turning Road at Montgeroult* (below), but you can see how Cézanne simplified the scene. He modelled the shapes of the houses, trees and sky in blocks of colour, organising them in layers on the flat picture canvas. They almost look like a set of cut-out pieces, stuck down on a surface. The Cubists liked that. Later they went on to use collage in their work.

BACK TO BASICS

Georges Braque took Cézanne's simple shapes and simplified them even more. In *Houses at L'Estaque* (right), the buildings and trees are reduced to bare geometric forms. Braque limited his colours further than Cézanne did, to just a few beiges, browns and greens. Like Cézanne, he showed his brushstrokes and left out any sign of a light source. The three dimensions of the real world are squashed down flat.

GRADUAL ABSTRACTION

Dutch artist Piet Mondrian thought in a similar way to the Cubists. At first he sketched from nature, but over the years he persistently stripped out detail. He merged shapes and flattened planes until he was left with a basic colour grid. This abstract style had begun with Cézanne, but moved a long way from the earlier artist's loyalty to painting what he could actually see.

Houses at L'Estaque, Georges Braque, 1908

 ART SPOT *Mondrian developed his style gradually, until he lost all representational detail. Can you see how he reached this point, using Cézanne's work and Cubism as a springboard? Try sketching an outdoor scene, then slowly breaking it down to basic blocks.*

Composition with Red, Blue and Yellow, Mondrian, 1921

POSING PEOPLE

While Cézanne was forward-thinking, he never forgot the art of the past. From the late 1880s, he began painting figures that were inspired by traditional themes. Unlike portraits, these works showed unnamed people who posed for him as models. They combined classic ideas with a striking modern feel.

SORROWFUL CLOWN

The diamond-patterned costume of the Harlequin had appealed to artists since the 18th century. Cézanne showed this theatrical joker in an unexpected way – alone and looking melancholy. The face is blurred to a mask-like state and the pose is almost paralysed. Cézanne's patchy background shows just a hint of a curtain that suggests the setting is a stage.

Harlequin, 1888–1890

ITALIAN PEASANT

On a visit to his Paris studio, Cézanne painted a young Italian model dressed in traditional peasant clothes. The pose, with one hand resting on a tilted hip, had been used by artists for centuries. But Cézanne broke the mould with his kaleidoscope background and the strange shafts of colour in the boy's face. The model looks lost in thought – a trademark of Cézanne's figure paintings at the time. You can spot traces of what was to become Cubism in the broken, hard-to-read shapes of the background.

Boy in a Red Waistcoat, 1888–1890

Mystical Head: Head Ascona, Alexej von Jawlensky, 1918

WILD BEASTS

Cézanne's daring colours, like the greens and purples in the face of the Italian boy, inspired a group of artists nicknamed the Fauves ('wild beasts'). Led by Henri Matisse (see p.17) and André Derain (1880–1954), they painted with fierce brushstrokes and extreme, often unnatural colours that distracted from the subject of the painting. Alexej von Jawlensky (1864–1941) exhibited with the Fauves. In the above painting of a girl's face, you can see how his colours sparked emotions like Expressionist paintings (see p.21) did.

THE CARD PLAYERS

Back in Provence, Cézanne used servants, peasants and workmen from his local village as models. They became the inspiration for one of his most famous sets of paintings – *The Card Players*. He painted at least five versions.

PREPARATION

Cézanne made more sketches and studies for this series than for any other work. They all show single figures that he would later group together in a scene. Many, such as *The Smoker* (below) are important paintings in their own right. This one almost looks like a portrait, though there's nothing personal about it.

The Card Players, 1890–1892

  ART SPOT *Compare this version of* The Card Players *to the later one opposite. Which elements have been lost? How has Cézanne changed the scene?*

TRADITIONAL THEME

The card-playing theme was inspired by a 17th-century painting that Cézanne saw in a museum in Aix. Genre painting, or showing ordinary people in everyday settings, had emerged in northern Europe at around that time. But Cézanne's work was different from his predecessors'. Instead of painting people interacting in a lively way, his figures look motionless and detached.

The Smoker, c.1890–1892

The Card Players, 1892–1895

PARING DOWN

Cézanne didn't add detail as he worked through the series – in fact, he did the reverse. The first paintings include three card players with spectators, while the last show just two men with cards. Cézanne's brushstrokes become vaguer until they reveal only the bare essentials. In the final composition, the players have little to distract them but their cards.

MODERN INTEREST

Many modern artists have paid homage to Cézanne's *The Card Players*, including the avant-garde Kazimir Malevich (1879–1935), the Cubist Fernand Léger (1881–1955) (see p.43) and contemporary Canadian photographer, Jeff Wall (1946–). They each picked elements of Cézanne's composition or style and adapted them in their own way. In 2011, one of Cézanne's *The Card Players* sold to a private collector for over US$250 million – the most ever paid for a painting at the time.

DARKNESS AND LIGHT

By the 1890s, Cézanne was spending so much time alone in Provence that one critic wondered if he was still alive! His isolation shows in some sombre figure paintings from this period. But while he hid away in the south of France, Cézanne's work began to earn new respect in Paris.

LONELY FIGURE

The ageing Cézanne seems to feel sympathy for this hunched figure of an elderly former nun (below). She emerges from dark shadows, anxiously clutching her rosary beads and as isolated as the man who painted her. A friend of Cézanne's found this painting on his studio floor, beneath a pipe dripping water. Perhaps this shows that the artist still lacked faith in his work.

An Old Woman with Rosary, 1895

SOLO SHOW

The art dealer Ambroise Vollard (1866–1939) took a shine to Cézanne's work after seeing it in a Paris paint shop. In 1895, he staged an exhibition in the capital – Cézanne's first solo show. The reclusive artist refused to go, but he sent along 150 paintings. They won praise among fellow artists, if not the general public.

PATIENT POSING

When Vollard sat for a portrait by Cézanne, he was ordered to stay still, 'like an apple'! After endless weeks of posing, he noticed two small unpainted patches on his hands.

ART SPOT *Can you see the bare spots of canvas on Vollard's hand? Cézanne never did finish this painting.*

Portrait of Ambroise Vollard, 1899

Portrait of Ambroise Vollard, Pablo Picasso, c.1910

When he pointed this out, Cézanne replied, 'maybe I shall find the right shade tomorrow... if I were to just put any random colour there I would be compelled to overpaint my entire picture.' Poor Vollard shuddered at the thought.

VISIONS OF VOLLARD

Vollard helped many other artists at the time, including Pablo Picasso. In this Cubist portrait, Picasso shows Vollard's importance by drawing attention to his head, which explodes across the canvas as if it is bulging with brains.

FRAGMENTED FORMS

Towards the end of his life, Cézanne's style became increasingly loose and fragmented. His hatched brushstrokes started to look more dramatic and unrestrained. Even so, he hung onto his sense of balance and order, thinking carefully before he placed down each patch of paint.

BLOCKY ROCKS

Now in his 60s, Cézanne continued to trek into the countryside. He had grown fascinated by an abandoned quarry not far from Mont Sainte-Victoire, and rented a cabin there to store his canvases. The craggy landscape perfectly suited his geometric style. He was inspired by the bright reddish-yellow rock, which he dismantles (right) until it almost merges with the trees.

Corner of Bibemus Quarry, 1900–1902

Mont Sainte-Victoire from Les Lauves, 1904–1906

MELTING MOUNTAIN

In *Mont Sainte-Victoire from Les Lauves*
(opposite, bottom), it gets harder to distinguish
between the plain, mountain and sky. Colours
are echoed around the canvas and patches are
deliberately left bare. Cézanne scattered cool
blues to create a sense of air, and warm reds
and yellows for shimmering light. The scene
feels unsettled yet permanent at the same time.

ART SPOT *Notice the swatches of green in the
sky and blue in the landscape of* Mont
Sainte-Victoire from Les Lauves. *What
effect does this have on the scene?*

PATCHWORK MAP

Painter and printmaker Jasper Johns
(1930–) must have remembered Cézanne's
broken brushstrokes when he created *Map*
(below). It shows the shape of the USA, roughly
keeping the states' proportions, but abstracting
them. Johns splashed paint across this huge
canvas in a chaotic, energetic way. He didn't
try to mimic a real map, just as Cézanne
didn't try to mimic nature.

Map, Jasper Johns, 1961

MASTER OF WATERCOLOUR

The freer feeling of Cézanne's late landscapes also shows in his hundreds of watercolours. Using this fast-drying paint, he couldn't change and rework things as he did with stickier oils. Cézanne's watercolours look quick and spontaneous – though that's not entirely the case!

METHODICAL WORK

Cézanne was as methodical as ever in creating his watercolours, letting each dab dry before adding another. He began with the shadows, slowly building up tints of colour until the object took shape. Just as important was the bare white paper, which Cézanne used to create passages of light. It often shines through in huge patches, giving the paintings a fragile feel.

Forest Path, c.1904-1906

PENCIL AND PAINT

In many of Cézanne's watercolours you can see clear pencil lines. Traditional painters would colour in the lines – but here they often take their own course. In places it looks as if Cézanne has changed his mind about a shape, or his floating flashes of paint have escaped their outlines. In others the silvery pencil is scribbled across coloured areas like shading. Sometimes it is hard to tell if Cézanne drew the pencil lines first or last.

 ART SPOT *Cézanne's airy watercolours influenced his oil paintings around this time. Compare these pictures to the landscapes on the previous page and the bathers on p.40. What are the similarities, and how do they feel different?*

Montagne Sainte–Victoire from Les Lauves, 1902–1906

SPOOKY SKULLS

Skulls were a popular subject with Cézanne. Here they sit on a decorative cloth. They stare out spookily towards us, with pencil lines indicating their dents and curves. The pattern on the cloth seems to echo the wiggly shapes of the skulls' eyes and jaws.

DIFFERENT STYLE

Cézanne's technique differed from many watercolour artists, who often blend paint while it is wet. JMW Turner (1775–1851) used this approach to create subtle light effects, as you can see in *The Red Rigi* (below). Turner, like Cézanne, wanted to stay true to nature without copying it.

Three Skulls, 1902–1906

The Red Rigi, JMW Turner, 1842

THE LARGE BATHERS

Cézanne created over 200 paintings and drawings of bathers in his lifetime. Males, females, single figures and groups – they're all nude or semi-nude figures in a landscape. In his final years, he worked on three huge canvases that became some of his best-known and most influential works.

TWISTING TRADITION

The tradition of painting nudes in a landscape goes back to ancient myths and legends of gods and goddesses. Cézanne studied mythological works by artists such as Rubens (1577–1640) and Titian (c.1488–1576) in the Louvre, making endless copies of them. He borrowed elements of their poses and compositions, but his style is entirely different. Any sense of human beauty and the softness of flesh, and crucially, any idea of myth or storytelling, is gone.

EVOLVING SCENE

Cézanne spent eight years working on *The Large Bathers*. Even so, it has an unfinished feel. White canvas glares through, and in places bodies merge with the sky or trees. The soft blues and ochres are shared around the scene so that skin, air and earth seem to be made of the same thing. Cézanne was as interested in negative space around the figures as he was in the figures themselves. This was something that Matisse (opposite), Mondrian (see p.29) and other abstract artists latched onto.

The Large Bathers, 1900–1906

The Dance, Henri Matisse, 1910

 **ART SPOT** *Some of the nudes in* The Large Bathers *(opposite) have shifting outlines or blurred forms. Why do you think this is? What effect does it have on the painting?*

ABSTRACT IMPACT

Cézanne's otherworldly bathers had a huge impact on modern artists. Henri Matisse owned an earlier version – in fact it was one of his most prized possessions. He and Picasso both went on to explore the world of abstract nudes, creating influential works of their own. When the sculptor Henry Moore (1898–1986) saw *The Large Bathers* in 1922, he said it was one of the most important moments of his life.

 **ART SPOT** *Like Cézanne, Matisse was interested in how his painting worked as a complete design. What similarities can you see between* The Dance *and* The Large Bathers *opposite? Think about the way both artists used colours and shapes.*

# FATHER OF US ALL

On 15 October, 1906, Cézanne set out in his usual way to paint, but he got caught in a storm and developed a chill that turned to pneumonia. He died a week later. The following year, a major exhibition of his work was held at the Paris Salon.

STEALING SECRETS

Matisse, Picasso and Braque were among the artists who went along to the exhibition to delve for Cézanne's secrets. Picasso called him 'My one and only master...the father of us all', while Matisse declared, 'If Cézanne is right, I am right.' Whether he knew it or not, Cézanne had changed the course of art history. Modern artists took what they could from him, and developed it in their own way.

NEVER SATISFIED

Ironically, Cézanne was never really happy with his achievements. He once said, 'I could paint for a hundred years, a thousand years without stopping and I would still feel as though I knew nothing.' Many people accused him of not being able to draw, or not understanding art. These things ended up being just what made him so important.

ART SPOT *Maurice Denis (1870–1943) painted a group of admiring artists gathered around a Cézanne painting (below). Do you recognise this still life from earlier in the book?*

Homage to Cézanne, Maurice Denis, 1900

LINKING PAST AND FUTURE

Cézanne shot to fame very suddenly after his death. People saw that he had built a bridge between the art of the past and the future. He set off a chain reaction that swung from Cubism and Fauvism to Expressionism and abstraction. Long since his lifetime, artists as varied as Fernand Léger, Alberto Giacometti (1901–1966) and Brice Marden (1938–) have thanked Cézanne for his brave and inspiring work.

The Card Players, Fernand Léger, 1917

ART SPOT *Léger took Cézanne's cylinders and cones to extremes in this Cubist image. How does it compare to* The Card Players *on p.32-33?*

TIMELINE

1839 Paul Cézanne is born in Aix-en-Provence, France.

1852 Cézanne starts at the Collège Bourbon school, where he meets Émile Zola.

1858 To please his father, he goes to university to study law. Alongside, he takes drawing classes.

1861 Encouraged by Zola and with his father's eventual consent, Cézanne enrols at a Paris art school. Here he is introduced to Camille Pissarro. After five months, he crumbles with self doubt and returns to Provence to work in his father's bank.

1862 Cézanne returns to Paris to study art again. From now on, he shifts back and forth between the capital and Aix.

1869 Cézanne meets Hortense Fiquet and lives with her in Paris.

1872 His son Paul is born and the family move to Pontoise. Cézanne paints outdoors with Pissarro.

1874 He shows three paintings in the first Impressionist exhibition. They are ridiculed by the critics.

1870 Cézanne retreats to the fishing village of L'Estaque in Provence, to avoid being enlisted in the Franco-Prussian War. He paints his first scene showing Mont Sainte-Victoire, the mountain that will captivate him over the coming decades.

1877 Again, his paintings get a terrible reception at the second Impressionist exhibition.

Cézanne paints *Madame Cézanne in a Red Armchair* – an early portrait of his future wife.

1879 Cézanne starts work on *Still Life with Compotier*, the first of many great still lifes from his mature period.

c1885 He paints *Bay of Marseilles, Seen from L'Estaque*. The coastline here had fascinated him since the 1870s.

1886 Zola publishes a novel about a failed artist, which appears to be based on Cézanne. The two fall out. In the same year, Cézanne marries Hortense and his father dies. He starts to spend more time alone in Provence.

1888 Cézanne begins a series of four costume pieces, including *Harlequin*, based on an Italian theatre style called *Commedia dell'arte*.

1890 He starts the first of five paintings of *The Card Players*.

1894 Cézanne begins a series of three large-scale *Bathers* paintings. He continues to work on them until the year of his death.

c1895 Cézanne paints two versions of *Still Life with Plaster Cupid*, an unusual subject choice for him.

1895 Art dealer Ambroise Vollard holds Cézanne's first solo exhibition in Paris.

1899 Ambroise Vollard sits for a portrait by Cézanne, which he never quite finishes.

1904 Cézanne is given a whole room at the Salon d'Automne exhibition.

1905 Matisse and other artists exhibit together and are named 'Fauves'.

1906 Cézanne dies of pneumonia in Aix.

1907 A successful retrospective of Cézanne's work is held in Paris. Picasso and Braque produce the first Cubist works.

2011 A version of *The Card Players* sells for over £170 million – in contrast to a work in 1890, which made the equivalent of around £16.

SELECTED WORKS

Background information on some of Cézanne's works:

MONT SAINTE-VICTOIRE WITH A LARGE PINE, 1887 (P.25)

Cézanne's Mont Sainte-Victoire paintings are great examples of the way he turned complicated detail into simple geometric designs. In the picture on page 25, everything has a sense of order. The tree branches follow the shape of the mountain, framing it and pointing us to it. We get a feeling of stability from the blocky houses and grid-like landscape, as well as Cézanne's uniform brushstrokes. Even the sky contains a pattern of colour that balances that of the ground below.

In a letter to his son, Cézanne once wrote: 'The same subject seen from a different angle offers subject for study of the most powerful interest and so varied that I think I could occupy myself for months without changing place, by turning now more to the right, now more to the left.' He was talking about the mountain that kept him fascinated for over 20 years.

KITCHEN TABLE (STILL LIFE WITH BASKET), 1888-1890 (P.26)

Still life subjects attracted Cézanne because he could control the exact content of each picture. The painting on page 26 is a complicated set-up, packed with geometric shapes and diagonal lines. There are lots of repeated curves, including the apples, pears and the loop of the ginger pot and basket. These contrast with the angular forms of the table, chair and canvases propped behind.

Everything on the table seems to jostle for space, so the still life doesn't really look still at all! At the same time, the white cloth ties the objects together and settles them in their place. Some things, like the wooden leg jutting in from the right, cast impossible shadows. Cézanne didn't want to paint a believable reality, but something that made us question and think about what we see.

THE CARD PLAYERS, 1890–1895 (P.32-33)

When Cézanne painted *The Card Players*, he took a traditional subject and launched it into his own world. He abandoned the light-hearted scenes of rowdy gamblers that had been popular since the 1600s, and anchored his figures like monumental statues. He didn't try to paint people literally, but blurred their faces and distorted their shapes so they suited his composition as a whole.

Look back to page 33 – the player smoking a pipe looks out of proportion, with a small head on a huge body and over-extended knees. The table tilts to the left, but the symmetry of the composition seems to balance this out. Cézanne also used colour to harmonise the scene, see-sawing cool blues and warm flesh tones across the canvas. Although the players look frozen in their game, he breathed life into them with his chunky brushstrokes that ripple across the picture's surface.

LARGE BATHERS, 1898–1905 (P.40)

We see more oddly shaped figures in *Large Bathers*. Cézanne didn't like working from life models – he based many of these nudes on drawings from his student days, some of which were copies of works in the Louvre. But far from the sensual nudes of traditional painting, his look almost clumsy and were declared ugly when people first saw them.

Of course Cézanne's strange shapes were deliberate – they all had to fit his painting's structure. The figures form a pyramid pattern that extends up through the leaning trees, and the broken colours help to lead our eye around the scene. The canvas measures 2.10 x 2.51 metres, on the scale of a huge historical painting, but the setting and style is modern. What are the nudes doing here? We don't know, because story wasn't a concern for Cézanne.

There's another break from tradition in the way the painting is finished – Cézanne wasn't afraid to let lines and bare canvas show. He was very aware that the edges of curved things like human bodies and apples aren't actual edges, just points where the object disappears from view. You can see how he searched for ways to depict this in the dissolved and shifting forms.

abstract not representing an actual object, place or living thing. Abstract art often focusses on basic shapes, lines, colours or use of space

avant-garde introducing new and experimental ideas in art

canvas a strong type of fabric that many artists use to paint on, especially in oils

collage pieces of paper, fabric or other materials, that are stuck onto a surface to create a picture

complementary colours colours that have maximum contrast between each other. The basic pairs for artists are red and green, blue and orange, and yellow and purple

composition the arrangement of parts of a picture

contemporary living in our time – or the same time as someone else (Cézanne's contemporaries included Claude Monet and Camille Pissarro)

Cubism an art style (1907–1920s) in which artists, led by Pablo Picasso and Georges Braque, made images using simplified shapes and multiple viewpoints

easel a wooden stand that supports and artist's canvas or drawing board

Expressionism an art style (1905–1920s) in which artists tried to convey different emotions, often through exaggerated colours or distorted shapes

Fauve French for 'wild beast'. The nickname given to the artists, such as Henri Matisse, painting between about 1905–10 in very bright and clashing colours unrelated to the actual subjects of their pictures

foreground the part of a scene that is nearest to the viewer

genre painting painting scenes of everyday life and ordinary people, usually in a realistic or comical way. It became popular in the Netherlands in the 16th century and spread to the rest of Europe in the 1600s

geometric based on mathematical shapes such as the triangle, circle or sphere

impasto using paint thickly so that it stands out from the picture surface

Impressionism an art style (c1874–76) in which artists such as Claude Monet painted mostly outdoors, capturing fleeting moments and changing light using vivid colours and dappled brushstrokes

landscape in painting, usually a countryside scene

ochre a brownish yellow

oil paint a thick paint made with ground pigment and a drying oil such as linseed oil

Old Masters the great artists who worked in Europe between about 1400 and 1800. They included Titian, Rembrandt and Leonardo da Vinci

palette a board that artists mix their colours on. The word is also used to describe the range of colours in a painting

palette knife a flat, spatula-like knife used for mixing or applying paint

perspective the art of showing three-dimensional objects on a flat surface, creating the effect of depth or distance. Linear perspective involves a vanishing point on the horizon that everything leads towards

picture plane the two-dimensional surface of a painting

pigment any material, natural or produced chemically, used to give paints their colour

plein air a French expression meaning 'open air', used to describe the act of painting outdoors

portrait a painting, drawing or other artwork depicting a particular person

Post Impressionists the name later given to artists (1880s–c.1900) who took on elements of Impressionism but rejected others. They included Cézanne, Vincent van Gogh and Paul Gauguin

print any image, whether a reproduction or original, that can be produced in several identical copies. Before the invention of lithographs and photography, prints were normally created by either incising lines, usually in metal, or by carving out spaces in a wooden block

representational showing the physical appearance of something

retrospective an exhibition that looks back over the whole of an artist's work

Salon an official art exhibition in Paris, held yearly or twice yearly from 1737. It favoured traditional artists of the time, but was later joined by more progressive rivals such as the Salon d'Automne

sculptor a maker of three-dimensional art, called sculpture, which may include carving, modeling or casting

self-portrait an image that an artist makes of him or herself

still life an art work mainly featuring an arrangement of objects in the foreground, traditionally flowers, fruit and household items

spontaneous done in a natural and often sudden way, without forward thinking or planning

studio an artist's indoor workplace

texture in painting, the way different materials seem to reflect, absorb or transmit light; a suggestion of how they feel to the touch

three dimensional having or appearing to have depth as well as width and height

two dimensional flat, or lacking depth

vibrant bright and lively

watercolour a water-soluble paint that dries quickly and has a transparent effect when applied in thin layers, called washes

INDEX

FURTHER INFORMATION

BOOKS:

This is Cézanne by Jorella Andrews (Lawrence King Publishing 2015)
Great Artists of the World: Paul Cézanne by Alix Wood (Franklin Watts 2015)
In the Picture with Paul Cézanne by Iain Zaczek (Wayland 2014)
Cézanne: Masters of Art by Roberat Bernabei (Prestel 2013)

WEBSITES:

A site dedicated to Cézanne's work: **www.paul-cezanne.org**
Discover Cézanne's home, studio and other surroundings in Provence: **www.cezanne-en-provence.com/?lang=en**
Learn about Cézanne and his paintings at London's National Gallery: **www.nationalgallery.org.uk/artists/paul-cezanne**
Scroll down to Cézanne's name to read about several of his works: **www.musee-orsay.fr/en/collections/works-in-focus/painting.html**